Peace, Be Still

A COLORING BOOK FOR
REDISCOVERING REST AND SERENITY

Ink &
Willow

Peace, Be Still

Trade Paperback ISBN 978-0-593-23453-2

Cover and book design by Jessie Kaye
Cover illustration by Jennifer Tucker

Published in the United States by WaterBrook, an imprint of Random House, a division of Penguin Random House LLC.

Ink & Willow and its colophon are registered trademarks of Penguin Random House LLC.

Printed in the United States of America

2021—First Edition

2nd Printing

Special Sales
Most WaterBrook and Ink & Willow books are available at special quantity discounts when purchased in bulk by corporations, organizations, and special-interest groups. Custom imprinting or excerpting can also be done to fit special needs. For information, please email specialmarketscms@penguinrandomhouse.com.

COLOR YOUR WAY TO A DEEPER, MORE FULFILLING SENSE OF INNER PEACE

Peace I leave with you; my peace I give you. I do not give to you as the world gives.
Do not let your hearts be troubled and do not be afraid.

—JOHN 14:27

It's one thing to read this statement Jesus delivered to his disciples just hours before his arrest and crucifixion, but it's quite another to truly believe it. After all, we all probably understand on a basic, objective level that God has given us access to an unending supply of peace. Yet somehow that knowledge tends to get lost on its way to our hearts—mainly because experiencing true peace in our minds, souls, and daily practice is often easier said than done.

We may not be living under the totalitarian Roman Empire, as the disciples were when they were given this command, but we certainly are no strangers to hardship, struggles, and suffering. Due to the constant twenty-four-hour news cycle, the amount of suffering and injustice occurring at a global level, and the incessant and inescapable barrage of information and insults and inaccuracies on social media, grasping and maintaining a true sense of peace and tranquility can often feel elusive and even completely out of reach. But God's promises are not given only to be taken away. And thus his promise of peace is just as true now as it was 2,000 years ago. Once one realizes the real horrors and injustices that existed in that time, this command of "Do not let your hearts be troubled and do not be afraid" sounds even more shocking. But that is what God calls us to do: *be at peace in the midst of the storm.* In the midst of pain. In the midst of uncertainty.

In a way, the call to not let our hearts be troubled couldn't come in any other context. If things are going well—work running smoothly, finances balanced, children perfectly content, and relationships in alignment—the "be at peace" command would feel somewhat out of place. In other words, we don't need to be reminded to seek peace if all seems right with the world. We need this reminder when all seems lost, when all seems wrong, and when our grip on everything feels as intangible as sand slipping through our fingers. That is the exact moment when we need to tell our souls: *peace, be still.*

Wherever you might currently describe yourself on the scale of "having it all together" or "barely keeping it together," consider this coloring book your official gateway to reclaiming some of that inner peace you may have lost. As you meditate on the calming illustrations and life-giving words with a pen or pencil in hand, may you find yourself drawn back into the well of God's overflowing peace. And if internal worries or external distractions threaten to steal your newfound peace, feel free to engage with the "Peace, Be Still" Spotify playlist (link at the back of the book) while you color, meditate, and restore your soul.

If God could calm a raging sea with the words "Peace, be still," he can calm your raging thoughts and overwhelmed soul. So grab some pencils, queue up a peaceful playlist, give yourself space to breathe, and allow yourself to reclaim the peace that passes all understanding—the peace that God has promised you. Lastly, if you'd like to share some of your artwork and engage with other people using this book, post it on Instagram using the hashtag #PeaceBeStillColoringBook.

Don't give up when dark times come. The more storms you face in life, the stronger you'll be. Hold on. Your greater is coming.

—Germany Kent, author and broadcast journalist

Illustrated by Ann-Margret Hovsepian

You don't have to know what comes next. You only have to know that it is vital that you are here. That your breath must follow one another like storms & rainbows.

—Arielle Estoria, in her Instagram post from September 27, 2020

Illustrated by Laura Marshall Denny

The most important work can be birthed from the place where uncomfortable silence seeps between us. In those moments we're faced with the decision of whether to respond immediately with the assuredness of our truth or to let the silence work in us. To feel the sadness and anger and grief. To be reminded that there's more at work in the story of the other and that perhaps true peace requires the sacrifice of our own beloved stances in the pursuit of greater justice.

—Ashlee Eiland, from Human(Kind): How Reclaiming Human Worth and Embracing Radical Kindness Will Bring Us Back Together (WaterBrook, 2020)

Illustrated by Jennifer Tucker

Serenity

is not peace from the storm,
but peace within the storm

Serenity is not peace from the storm, but peace within the storm.

—author unknown

Illustrated by Holly Camp

God designed the human machine to run on Himself. He Himself is the fuel our spirits were designed to burn, or the food our spirits were designed to feed on. There is no other. That is why it is just no good asking God to make us happy in our own way without bothering about religion. God cannot give us a happiness and peace apart from Himself, because it is not there. There is no such thing.

—C. S. Lewis, *in* The C. S. Lewis Collection: Signature Classics and Other Major Works *(HarperOne, 2017)*

Illustrated by Ann-Margret Hovsepian

Be still and
dream
in the arms
of our Maker

- Cole Arthur Riley

And as that near and present glory passes before us, let us take
hold of your mysterious rest, knowing that the answer to our
insecurities is not to do or say more to make you pleased with
us, but to be still and dream in the arms of our Maker.

—Cole Arthur Riley, from her Black Liturgies Instagram post on October 18, 2020

Illustrated by Holly Camp

ANXIETY does not empty tomorrow of its SORROWS but it empties Today of its STRENGTH. ~ Alexander Maclaren ~

To-morrow will have its cares, spite of anything that anxiety and forboding can do. It is God's law of Providence that a man shall be disciplined by sorrow; and to try to escape from that law by any forecasting prudence is utterly hopeless, and madness. And what does your anxiety do? It does not empty to-morrow, brother of its sorrows; but, ah! it empties to-day of its strength. It does not make you escape the evil, it makes you unfit to cope with it when it comes. It does not bless to-morrow and it robs to-day.

—Alexander Maclaren, preached in the Union Chapel in Manchester, United Kingdom, in 1859

Illustrated by Bridget Hurley
Hand-lettered by Jennifer Tucker

Do not worry about tomorrow, for tomorrow will worry about itself.

MATTHEW 6:34

Do not worry about tomorrow, for tomorrow will worry about itself. Each day has enough trouble of its own.

—*Matthew 6:34*

Illustrated by Laura Marshall Denny

"When storms surround, and only clouds I see, Lord, be my comfort and ABIDE WITH ME."

-Emma Dietrich

Abide With Me

Abide with me; I need Thee every day,
To lead me on thro' all the weary way;
When storms surround, and only clouds I see,
Lord, be my comfort, and abide with me.

Be with me, Lord, where'er my path may lead;
Fulfill Thy word, supply my every need;
Help me to live each day more close to Thee,
And, oh, dear Lord, I pray, abide with me.

Abide with me, my Lord, and when at last,
This earth and all its weary cares are past;
I'll pray no more that Thou abide with me,
For then, at last, I shall abide with Thee.

—*Emma Graves Dietrich, 1904*

Illustrated by Jennifer Tucker

These things I have spoken to you, that in me you may have peace. In the world you will have trouble, but take heart, I have overcome the world.

—John 16:33

Illustrated by Laura Marshall Denny

I in my Savior am happy and blest

• FRANCES J. CROSBY •

Blessed Assurance

Blessed assurance, Jesus is mine!
Oh, what a foretaste of glory divine!
Heir of salvation, purchase of God,
Born of His Spirit, washed in His blood.

Perfect submission, perfect delight,
Visions of rapture now burst on my sight;
Angels descending, bring from above
Echoes of mercy, whispers of love.

Perfect submission, all is at rest,
I in my Savior am happy and blest;
Watching and waiting, looking above,
Filled with His goodness, lost in His love.

REFRAIN
   This is my story, this is my song,
   Praising my Savior all the day long;
   This is my story, this is my song,
   Praising my Savior all the day long

—*Frances J. Crosby (1820–1915), who was blind, wrote "Blessed Assurance" after hearing her friend play a new melody on the piano. The song is based on an interpretation of Hebrews 10:22.*

Illustrated by Laura Marshall Denny

When I say it's you I like, I'm talking about that part of you that knows that life is far more than anything you can ever see or hear or touch. That deep part of you that allows you to stand for those things without which humankind cannot survive. Love that conquers hate, peace that rises triumphant over war, and justice that proves more powerful than greed.

—Fred Rogers (1928–2003), better known as Mister Rogers, was the host of the preschool television series Mister Rogers' Neighborhood from 1968 to 2001. Mister Rogers, who dedicated his life to understanding children, was also a minister.

Illustrated by Jennifer Tucker

your peace is
a result of

radical
acceptance

of your life

— Glo Atanmo

Your peace is a result of radical acceptance of your life, your choices, and your circumstances, no matter what state they're in.

—Glo Atanmo, in her Glo Graphics Instagram post on September 30, 2020

Illustrated by Holly Camp

There is nothing like staying at home for real comfort.

—Jane Austen, in Emma (1815). Austen (1775–1817) was an English novelist who wrote about ordinary people in everyday life in her novels, which remain popular classics two centuries after her death.

Illustrated by Bridget Hurley
Hand-lettered by Ann-Margret Hovsepian

Deceit is in the heart of those who devise evil,
but those who plan peace have joy.

—Proverbs 12:20

Illustrated by Ann-Margret Hovsepian

Go carry
thy burden
to Jesus

-H.J. Zelley

Carry It All to Jesus

O what is thy burden so heavy today,
That gloom fills thy spirit and joy flees away?
Thy faults rise before thee and fill with dismay,
Go carry thy burden to Jesus.

O what is thy burden so maketh thee weep,
That clouds the bright sunlight and banishes sleep?
Thy failures have caused thee this anguish so deep,
Go carry thy burden to Jesus.

O what is thy burden so great and severe,
That like a great thunder cloud hovers so near-
Thy fears and forebodings both gloomy and drear?
Go carry thy burden to Jesus.

O what is thy burden so presses again,
That long like a blight on thy spirit hath lain?
Thy friends who are wandering have caused thee this pain,
Go carry thy burden to Jesus.

CHORUS
  Carry thy burden to Jesus,
  Carry thy burden to Jesus,
  Thy faults and thy failures, Thy friends and thy fears
  He'll carry each burden, and wipe away tears,
  Go carry thy burden to Jesus.

— H. J. Zelley (1859–1942) became a Methodist minister in 1882 and retired
in 1929. He produced more than 1,500 poems, hymns, and gospel songs.

Illustrated by Holly Camp

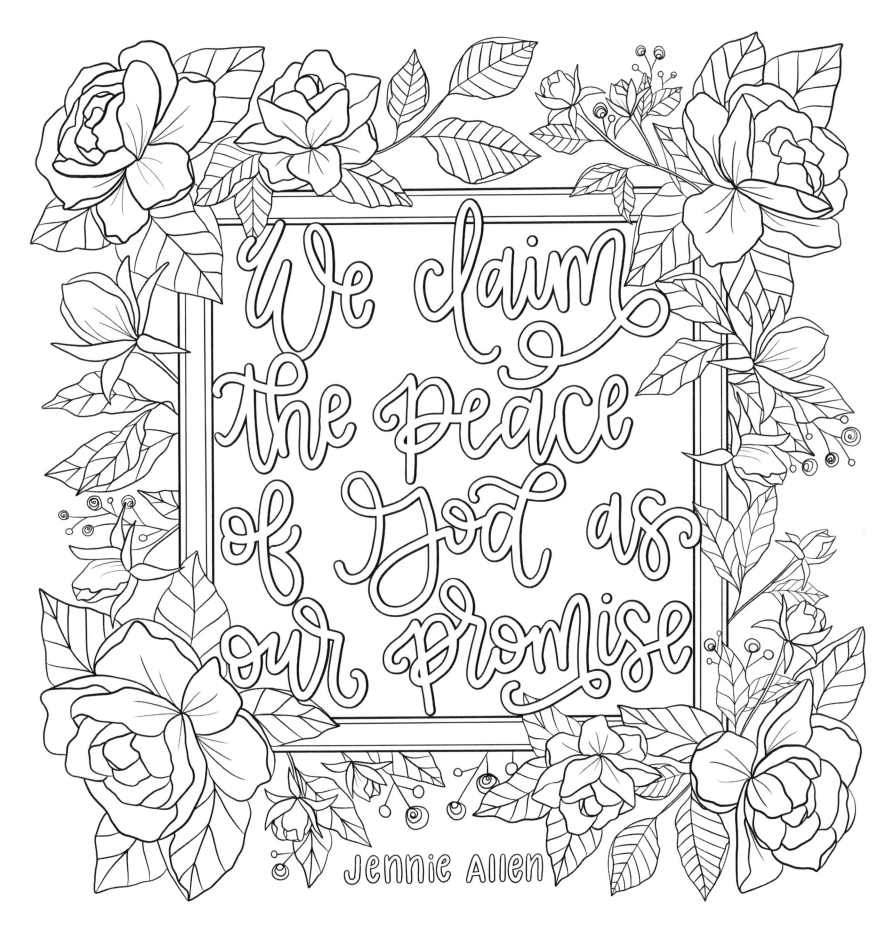

We claim the peace of God as our promise

Jennie Allen

We claim the peace of God as our promise.

—Jennie Allen, in Get Out of Your Head: Stopping the Spiral of Toxic Thoughts *(WaterBrook, 2020)*

Illustrated by Laura Marshall Denny

hold only love, only place in your heart.

John Lewis

Release the need to hate, to harbor division, and the enticement of revenge. Release all bitterness. Hold only love, only peace in your heart, knowing that the battle of good to overcome evil is already won.

—John Lewis, in Across That Bridge: Life Lessons and a Vision for Change *(Hachette, 2012). Lewis (1940–2020), one of the "Big Six" leaders of the civil rights movement in the 1960s. Lewis led more than 600 marchers across the Edmund Pettus Bridge in Selma, Alabama, in 1965, a demonstration march that became known as "Bloody Sunday" because of the brutal attacks by law enforcement.*

Illustrated by Jennifer Tucker

God often speaks loudest when we're quietest.

—Mark Batterson, in Whisper: How to Hear the Voice of God (WaterBrook, 2017)

Illustrated by Ann-Margret Hovsepian

Forgiveness is a healing balm. It's the way to freedom, the way to peace.

—Latasha Morrison, in Be the Bridge: Pursuing God's Heart for Racial Reconciliation (WaterBrook, 2019)

Illustrated by Laura Denny

One day we must come to see that peace is not merely a distant goal that we seek, but a means by which we arrive at that goal. We must pursue peaceful ends through peaceful means.

—Martin Luther King Jr., in a 1967 speech on the casualties of the war in Vietnam

Illustrated by Bridget Hurley
Hand-lettered by Ann-Margret Hovsepian

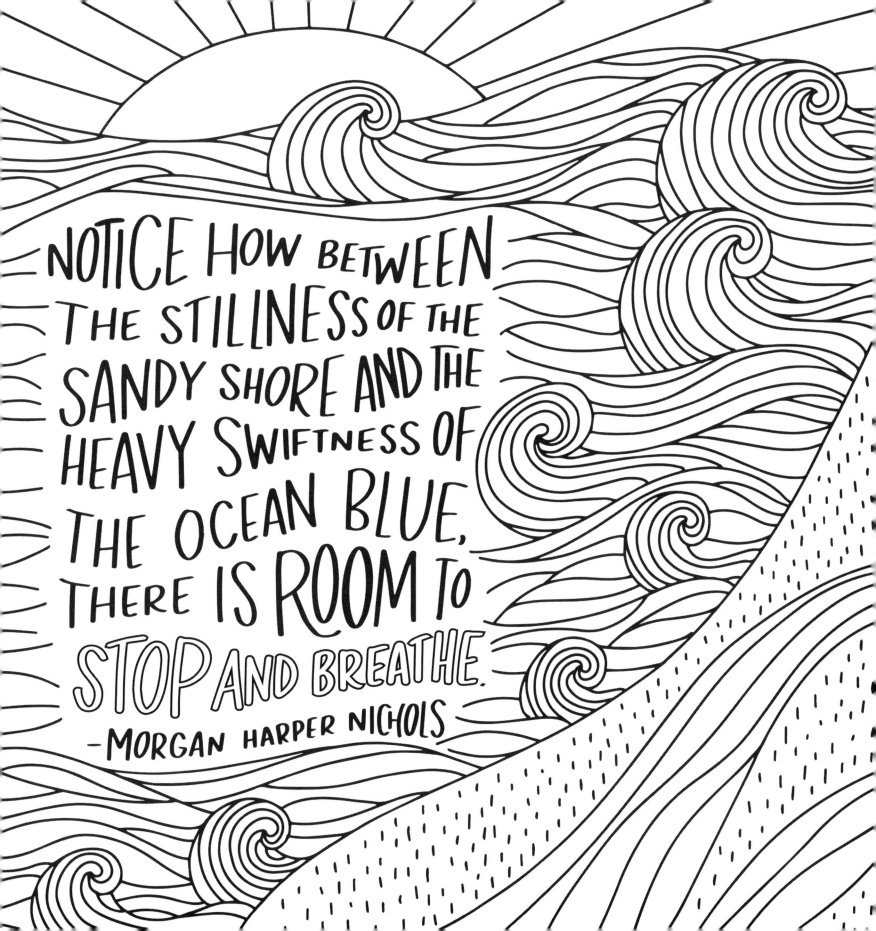

On this journey into the depths, you are free to take your time. You are free to pace yourself no matter how crowded your mind. Notice how between the stillness of the sandy shore and the heavy swiftness of the ocean blue, there is room to stop and breathe and let the sun fall down on you reminding you: no matter your pace you will grow how you were meant to.

—Morgan Harper Nichols, in an Instagram post, October 29, 2020

Illustrated by Jennifer Tucker

You will keep him in perfect peace, whose mind is stayed on you, because he trusts in you.

—Isaiah 26:3

Illustrated by Ann-Margret Hovsepian

Bring peace
to others

- Thomas à Kempis

First keep peace with yourself; then you will be able to bring peace to others.

—Thomas à Kempis (1380–1471), in The Imitation of Christ (1418–1427),
one of the most widely read Christian works on devotion

Illustrated by Holly Camp

Then He arose and rebuked the wind, and said to the sea, "Peace, be still!" And the wind ceased and there was a great calm.

—Mark 4:39 (NKJV)

Illustrated by Holly Camp

There is PEACE even in the STORM

VINCENT VAN GOGH

My peace I leave with you—we saw how there is peace even in the storm. Thanks be to God who has given us to be born and to live in a Christian country.

—Vincent Van Gogh, in a letter to his brother, Theo, November 3, 1876

Illustrated by Jennifer Tucker

fear not
for I am with you

- Isaiah 41:10

Fear not, for I am with you; be not dismayed, for I am your God;
I will strengthen you, I will help you, I will uphold you with my
righteous right hand.

— Isaiah 41:10 (NKJV)

Illustrated by Holly Camp

Lord, make me an instrument of your peace; where there is hatred, let me sow love; where there is injury, pardon; where there is discord, union; where there is doubt, faith; where there is despair, hope; where there is darkness, light; and where there is sadness, joy.

—Although this prayer is often attributed to St. Francis of Assisi, its origins are actually unknown. The prayer is believed to have been written in the early twentieth century, long after the life of Francis in the twelfth century.

Peace I leave with you, my peace I give to you;
not as the world gives do I give to you. Let not
your heart be troubled, neither let it be afraid.

—John 14:27

Illustrated by Bridget Hurley
Hand-lettered by Ann-Margret Hovsepian

After a storm comes a calm.

—Matthew Henry (1662–1714). Henry was an English clergyman who is best known for the six-volume biblical commentary Exposition of the Old and New Testaments.

Illustrated by Bridget Hurley
Hand-lettered by Ann-Margret Hovsepian

Do not be anxious about anything, but in every situation, by prayer
and petition, with thanksgiving, present your requests to God.
And the peace of God, which transcends all understanding,
will guard your hearts and your minds in Christ Jesus.

—Philippians 4:6–7

Illustrated by Ann-Margret Hovsepian

The path of peace comes only when we're willing to walk into our own darkness & face our own shadows.

ERWIN MCMANUS

The path of peace comes only when we're willing to walk
into our own darkness and face our own shadows.

—*Erwin McManus, in* The Way of the Warrior: An Ancient Path to Inner Peace *(WaterBrook, 2019)*

Illustrated by Jennifer Tucker

HOW beautiful ON THE mountains ARE THE FEET OF THOSE WHO BRING good news.

ISAIAH 52:7

How beautiful on the mountains are the feet of those who bring good news, who proclaim peace, who bring good tidings, who proclaim salvation, who say to Zion, "Your God reigns!"

—Isaiah 52:7

Illustrated by Jennifer Tucker

Abound in hope

- Romans 15:13

May the God of hope fill you with all joy and peace in believing, so that by the power of the Holy Spirit you may abound in hope.

—Romans 15:13

Illustrated by Holly Camp

Peace can come both in the letting go and in the hanging on.

JENNIFER DUKES LEE

As you step out in faith, God's peace will prevail—and that peace
can come both in the letting go and in the hanging on.

—Jennifer Dukes Lee, in It's All Under Control: A Journey of Letting Go, Hanging On, and
Finding a Peace You Almost Forgot Was Possible (Tyndale, 2018)

Illustrated by Jennifer Tucker

We are able to be our best selves when we are centered in a place of quiet rest.

REBEKAH LYONS

We would do well to understand that we are able to be our
best selves when we are centered in a place of quiet rest.

—Rebekah Lyons, in Rhythms of Renewal: Trading Stress and Anxiety for a Life of Peace and Purpose (Zondervan, 2019)

Illustrated by Jennifer Tucker

The effect of
righteousness
will be

Peace

- Isaiah 32:17

The effect of righteousness will be peace, and the result of righteousness, quietness and trust forever.

—Isaiah 32:17

Illustrated by Holly Camp

TO *rest* IS TO CEASE STRIVING, TO BE *restored* AND *refreshed.*

• RUTH CHOU SIMONS •

To rest is to cease striving, to be restored and refreshed.

—Ruth Chou Simons, in Gracelaced: Discovering Timeless Truths
Through Seasons of the Heart (Harvest House, 2017)

Illustrated by Ann-Margret Hovsepian

Finally, brothers, rejoice. Aim for restoration, comfort one another, agree with one another, live in peace; and the God of love and peace will be with you.

—2 Corinthians 13:11

Illustrated by Laura Marshall Denny

All shall be well, and all shall be well, and absolutely everything shall be well.

—Julian of Norwich

Illustrated by Laura Marshall Denny

We slow down. Breathe. Come back to the present.

—*John Mark Comer, in* The Ruthless Elimination of Hurry: How to Stay Emotionally Healthy and Spiritually Alive in the Chaos of the Modern World *(WaterBrook, 2019)*

Illustrated by Jennifer Tucker

Anxiety weighs down the heart,
but a kind word cheers it up.

—Proverbs 12:25

Illustrated by Laura Marshall Denny

SOMETIMES IT TAKES A WRONG TURN TO GET YOU TO THE RIGHT PLACE.

♡MANDY HALE♡

Sometimes it takes a wrong turn to get you to the right place.

—Mandy Hale, blogger, author, and speaker

Illustrated by Ann-Margret Hovsepian

Breathe in His peace.

—The Joshua Centre. Visit joshuacentre.org.uk/breathe-confession for the full Breathe Confession.

Illustrated by Laura Marshall Denny

Artists, Illustrator, and Hand-Letterers

We'd like to give a big thank you to the following people for sharing their creativity on the pages of this book. We handed them the text and set them loose to illustrate it in their own unique styles. You can check out their websites, Etsy sites, and Facebook or Instagram pages to see more of their art and learn more about them.

Holly Camp

HollyCampCards.etsy.com

Bridget Hurley

BHurleyStudio.etsy.com

Laura Marshall Denny

DoodlingForDays.etsy.com

Ann-Margret Hovsepian

AnnHovsepian.com

Jennifer Tucker

LittleHouseStudio.net

Playlist

We truly want this book to help you engage in a rich worship experience and to be uplifting to your soul and spirit. Music speaks so much deeper than just words, so we've created a playlist of songs to listen to while you create your unique work of art. We know the result will be beautiful.

https://wmbooks.com/PeaceBeStill